TAO TE CHING

Lao-tzu

An
authentic
Taoist
translation

By Taoist Master John Bright-Fey

Book design by Miles G. Parsons and Pat Covert
Layout and graphic consulting by Charlie Fechter
Calligraphy copyright © 2004 John Bright-Fey

Printed in the U.S.

TABLE OF CONTENTS

INTRODUCTION

The *Tao Te Ching* is the fundamental text of both philosophic and religious Taoism. It was written during the "Spring and Autumn Classical Period" (700–480 BCE) by a native of the southern Chinese feudal state of *Ch'u* named *Li Erh*. According to legend, *Li Erh*, an imperial librarian, keenly observed the world around him, including the political intrigues of China's feudal lords. He recorded what he saw and employed ancient Shamanic rituals as a means of understanding the complexities of human interaction. Eventually, he distilled his lifetime of knowledge into a long poem written in the literary language of the period. This poem is the *Tao Te Ching*. Because it was filled with both ancient wisdom and the profound insight of a child, *Li Erh* became known as *Lao-tzu*, which combines the meanings of "old wise man" and "innocent child." Since then, Taoist mystics have referred to *Lao-tzu* as "The Ancient Child."

The *Tao Te Ching*: The Source and Its Effects

The poem known as the *Tao Te Ching* is composed of roughly 5,000 ancient Chinese characters arranged in archaic poetic form and rhyme scheme. Its language is at once cryptic, terse, and very beautiful and eloquent. Supposedly, it reflects the personality of *Lao-tzu* himself. In fact, many *Taoists* often refer to the poem simply as "The *Lao-tzu*." It describes the source of all life and existence *(Tao)* and the benevolent effects *(Te)* that the all-pervading source has on mankind. The poem itself is a complete classic body *(Ching)* of Chinese wisdom that has been studied by scholars for centuries. It stands as one of the most popular works in all of the world's great literature.

While there are many translations of the *Tao Te Ching* available, most of them simply deliver the cargo; that is to say, each accomplishes the task of translation with great care and smooth efficiency. However, the academic professionalism of the translator often gets between the reader and what is being read. This is an unavoidable consequence of translation from one language to another. Invariably, the personality and life experience of the translator will be reflected in the translation. While each of the available *Tao Te Ching* translations in English is wonderful in its own way, none of them adequately reflects the perspective of a practicing Taoist that has been initiated into the mystic tradition — that is, until now.

The *Tao Te Ching* you are about to read comes from the secret oral tradition of the *T'ien-Shih* or "Celestial Masters" sect of Taoism that combines elements of both the philosophic and religious schools. Also known as the *Wu-tou-mi Tao* ("Five Pecks of Rice School"), this sect maintains a private body of arcane Taoist rituals, meditation techniques, and mystic literature. Initiates in this school are charged with maintaining a continuous link with *Lao-tzu* himself in order that authentic Taoist wisdom of the past will always be available in the present. It is this wisdom that I want to share with you.

On this Translation

There is no direct way to substitute one English word for a single Chinese character. Instead, characters can represent many English words and concepts. The ancient Chinese language of the *Tao Te Ching* is a particularly complex and nuanced one that abounds with paradox. Additionally, a Chinese character has a depth of meaning with many subsidiary meanings "beneath" its predominant one. The language of the *Tao Te Ching* is context-oriented, wherein one of the character's minor meanings becomes the major, depending on what other characters are around it. This overlaps with Chinese poetic form and rhyme scheme, which allows for multiple interpretations of a block of characters. This would be akin to reading a paragraph in English not from the beginning to the end, but from the middle outward in a nonlinear way.

For this translation, I have chosen to exclude capital letters and used English punctuation only sparingly, since ancient Chinese contains neither. I have employed several neologisms that support authentic Taoist thinking. For example, the single word "bodymind" is intended to convey a deeper meaning than its constituent parts. Popular culture abounds with talk of reuniting the body with the mind. Taoist Cultivators, however, see no such separation to be remedied. That the body and mind form a unity is a foregone conclusion.

The choices of poetic structure are my own and reflect the long hours of recitation necessary to memorize the *Tao Te Ching*. They are also my attempts to translate ancient Chinese poetic forms into a contemporarily relevant structure for English readers.

I believe the world at large could benefit greatly from the authentic wisdom and knowledge contained in the *Tao Te Ching*. Yet so much of the conventional information about it obscures more than reveals. I humbly offer my own translation as a potential remedy to this situation. Now you will be able to journey into the Taoist heart and soul.

> *Let not your heart-mind be troubled*
> *Simply*
> *Flow into the Tao.*

>> — John Bright-Fey, Taoist Master
>> Reverend Venerable, *Tao-jen, Tao-shih*

CHAPTER ONE

the *tao* source of life that we often talk about
is beyond the power of words and labels to define or enclose

while it is true that we employ words and labels to outline our
experience
they are not absolute and cannot define the absolute

when it all began there were no words or labels

these things were created out of the union of preception and
perception

whether a person who is awake in play
sees the heart of life or its surface manifestations is hardly
important
because they are exactly the same point in space and time

the words and labels that we use make us think that they are
different
but only so we can talk about it from the outside of ourselves
in regard to the outside of the point in space and time

if you feel as though you really need a name
then call it the wonderwork
and watch one miracle talk to another
in a language that you can feel but not understand

it is playful to approach something that is logically
unknowable

CHAPTER TWO

as a matter of course

if you decide that something is beautiful
then something else immediately becomes ugly
without you realizing it

if you enter a thought shape that dictates the parameters of
what is a condition of health
then the parameters of a condition of unhealthy
come forward

you create death when you decide what constitutes life
you create difficulties when you create ease
you create long when you decide what is short
you create a low tone when you sing a high one

were you aware of the power of your own lifeforce

when looking to the left
different tones create harmony

whether you are truly clever or merely awake
manage your affairs without actions
and rely on fluid thinking rather than stagnant thought

adapt to conditions that present themselves
and remember that specialization
is not the useful way

continuously create instead of acquiring
and enjoy what you create

you are important only if it is not important to you

CHAPTER THREE

be wary of exalting the wise and sophisticated
for it becomes not unlike
pouring two liquids into a container meant for one

consider the relative wisdom of displaying treasures
that remain untouched in temporary keeping

authentic learning released through insight
nurtures the heart spirit
and does not disturb the balance

a sound leader helps the populace to be open minded and self
aware

with open heart spirits
strong bodyminds
even temperaments and thought clarity

these people make their own choices
and can naturally resist those meddling fools who try to steal their
ability
to respond

no force
no strain

natural action without deeds is the equilibrium of mankind

CHAPTER FOUR

the *tao* source of life is an empty vessel
vast within
vast without
possessed of transcendental space

it seems able to hold anything and everything

yet it is also a force

file down the sharpest edge with it

untie any knot and unknot any tangle

soften the harshest glare and settle unwanted dust

it is easy to secret away until needed
because it is already hidden away

but even in subtle storage
it seems to have a life all its own

nativity unknown
it was here before the parents of humanity
traversed the sky

CHAPTER FIVE

nature as creation is a relentless force

the relentless constantly faces the decay of its own fruits

the sound person also relentless
faces the decay of the fruits of mankind

in the midst of this unsentimental force there exists a mysterious space
the lungs and bellows of your universe

like lungs its shape changes
like bellows its function does not occur alone

the more that it works
the more that it brings forth

and words however eloquent
exhaust the magic of this sacred space

speak not in word or labels

you can only feel it with your core and viscera

CHAPTER SIX

the mysterious space is as silent and real as an imaginary
conversation

and yet

like a fertile valley
where two slopes meet
in conversation

the root of life takes hold to yield everything between
heaven and earth

enduring succession of continuous
interchanging

the mysterious space is always there
waiting for a director to use
its inexhaustible gossamer strength

CHAPTER SEVEN

look up
look down
look around

it has always been here

look up
look down
look around

it will always be here

infinite duration outlasting ordinary space and time

the universe that you perceive has always been here
and will be here after you are no longer present
to perceive it

because it gave birth to you and not the contrary to which you cling

rather than being one step ahead
and asleep towards up and coming possibilities

the sound traveler stays two steps back
and remains awake to all that is possible

if you look upon yourself as an accident in space and time

then you will always be present in space and time

it is as simple as finding yourself by not looking

this is a thought form for thinking into

Chapter Eight

if a person wants to be at their best
then they should pattern themselves after water

water serves the land and the life on the land

it gives this life by moving through the land
seeking its own balance and equilibrium

this is in contrast to human beings who always look up
and think of rising to some lofty achievement

water will always flow around obstacles
and seek out the lowest earthbound opened space that it can find

in this way
it is always closer to the miracle than we are

the miracle talks to us through water

and it says

wherever you choose to live remember
the earth beneath your feet
consider how to feel it with all that you do

whenever you want peace remember
to flow into your heartmind
plunging into the profound love that resides deep within you

however difficult remember
that you should speak frankly
but never drown others with your words

whichever instances call for leadership remember
that a constant stream helps order
the lifeforms around it

whatever business you transact remember
to go steadily to the source
and dutifully perform without washing up on unprepared land

if you listen to me
when there is a call to action
the miracle will tell you when it is time to act

contending causes contention

have no part of it
and you will be a cool stream
nourishing to all

CHAPTER NINE

pull an archer's bow past the limits of its construction
fill a gallon jug with two gallons of water
hone a knife to an excessively sharp edge
stretch overly a muscle towards achievement

all that you get is a
strained
dulled split
and broken
deformation of the miraculous

if you judge yourself by material things
that are temporarily in your possession
you will always be worried about who will take possession
of them next

if you are too proud of these material things
then you are courting personal disaster

the *tao* source of life has some advice for you

pause activity
enjoin with it
engage poise and relaxation

Chapter Ten

creative spirit
vital soul
wondrous bodymind

can you combine these into one phase
and gently hold onto it

one phase one part one moment

can you commune with
and direct the elemental force of life
and enter into the rebirth of gentleness
and be like a newborn

can you wash and cleanse your mystic inner vision
while clearing it of the refuse left behind by ordinary sight

is it possible for you to stay out of your own way
while being your own leader

can you stomp the earth
look to the heavens while being receptive
passive
possessed of quietude

can you be knowledgeable and clever
and regard it as whimsical

create and nourish
let all creation be the worlds
not your own

have fun when you work
work when you have fun

be a leader without appearing to be
and you will personify fine uncarved wood
in the hands of a master carpenter

can you guess who this master is

CHAPTER ELEVEN

here is a lesson for you

imagine thirty separate pieces of stick all cut to a uniform length

visualize the single sticks
and look at the two ends that are a part of each and every one of
them

end middle end

these thirty wooden sticks all have the power to unite to form the
hub of a
great wheel

in the process of this uniting
they give birth to the center of the hub

by sacrificing their individuality they magically create
the utility of the wheel

take a lump of clay and expand the enclosed center within
and a vessel is created

it is this expanded enclosure that makes the vessel useful

likewise a structure does not make a space and shape for living
space and shape are necessary for living

all of this is called creation through not-being

not-being creates the intangible

the intangible creates utility of the tangible

CHAPTER TWELVE

imagine a soft light of blue-green
imagine a strong red light
imagine a rich yellow light
imagine a bright white light
now imagine the black absence of color

if you look at these lights singly you will know what they are

if you allow them into your eyes all at once
then you will not be able to distinguish one from the other

the twelve musical notes can be arranged magically to create a
joyful noise

the twelve musical notes can also be thrown together without
method
like stones in a hole
that becomes an ordinary activity that denies the hole its usefulness

attempt to
eat something sour
eat something bitter
eat something sweet
eat something pungent
eat something salty
all at the same time and the once pleasant tastes are likely to
nauseate you

ordinary people exceed the basic goodness of the things of this
world
in searching for new ways to exceed themselves

the momentum of exceeding unbalances the heartmind
and generates insecurity and a loose footing that denies the true self

for these reasons
the sound person speaks to the unconscious heartmind

requesting instructions on how to nourish the true self

when gently asked
the unconscious teaches appreciation for those things that are
within us

all

when gently asked
the unconscious teaches circumspection for those things that are
without us

all

CHAPTER THIRTEEN

life and death
favor and disgrace
praise and blame
success and failure

all of these conditions confuse and dismay us because
they are the same ailment
they cause ill at ease states and related worries

how does this happen

when favor is acquired so is the fear of losing favor acquired

if someone thinks that the corporeal body is the limit of the self
then the fear that is inherent in the body makes itself known
and is difficult to subdue

how can you trust and accept your corporeal limits in the face of
fear

we have fear when a limited self is absorbed in importance

if you view the unlimited world as the self
then you can be trusted with it

because only the person who sees the world as themselves
and their self as the world

will take care of it

CHAPTER FOURTEEN

talking about the character of the *tao* source of life is fundamentally useless
talking about the lessons of the *tao* way of life is likewise useless

because the real way is a revealed way

awakened in yourself
only through an imitation
of the way
as yourself

but where are the clues to this awakening

look all around yourself deliberately
and attempt to see the nothing that is
deliberately all around yourself

nothing no thing nothing

if you cannot see it
then you are in its presence

try to listen deliberately
to the space between the sounds
of your deliberate world

if you do not hear anything
then you will be hearing it through its absence

grab hold of something with your hand and let it go
now imagine some things that you cannot grab with either your
hand or mind
then you will surely be holding it

invisible inaudible intangible

the form and function of these three components blend together
creating the *tao* way of life

do not think of it as upper and lower or dark and bright or rise and sink
instead view the miracle as something that is continuously moving
unnamable and totally elusive

it is a formless form and a methodless method
that gives birth to an image of no thing

when you confront it
there is no face to look at

when you pursue it
there is no shape to follow

it does not *tao* talk
it does not *tao* act

but if you look for the wisdom that it leaves in its wake
and deal with present realities accordingly

then you will have seized the beginning moment
that is the *tao* way of living

CHAPTER FIFTEEN

sage wise men of ancient space and time
were agents of the *tao* source of life
and as such appeared mysterious and intent
as they perceived the sacred voices and the subtle clues
of the miracle and its injunctions

their trance of wisdom was so profound
that they seem distant and removed
yet present and intrigued
as they gave their full attention
to observe the smallest of happenings
and while this behavior was beyond ordinary understanding
it can be described without looking to the mind

calculating yet spontaneous
a revealed attentiveness of a hunter crossing a frozen stream

fearless yet tentative
they behaved as if the teacher's teacher had placed a knife at every
quarter to keep them alert and aware

dignified yet playful
they conducted themselves as if to be the courteous guest of
everyone that they met

humble yet resolute
they deferred to the ordinary forces around them without
submission and looked like ice yielding in the sun

authentic and unspoiled
they acted with honest simplicity as if the depth of their beings
were composed of concentrated innocence

receptive and approachable
they presented a rarefied space of sanctuary and repose inviting to
all

carefree and gently demanding
they blended freely with nature and with people but did not
sacrifice their own inner direction

the ancient child asks
who is it that can find quiet among the noise

the sage wise man sits comfortably still
and can lay down amidst the confusion

the ancient child asks
who is it that can remain calm and seize the moment

through engaged activity the sage wise man preserves his life and
the life around him

to embrace the *tao* way of life is to seek emptiness
as a means to avoiding spiritual materialism
and the entropy it induces

by not seeking accomplishment
you become endless and vitalized
continually

CHAPTER SIXTEEN

deliver all your inner confusion to the earth
and resting quietly
leave your mind undisturbed

allow all things that manifest and their roots
to assume definite shape
and move about in activity
against the backdrop of your reflective awareness
and observe these events passively with a controlled heart and
simple spirit

when these bustling shapes slow down and cease in their activity
and return to the nothingness from whence they came
you will attain a state of quietude
that is an imitation of the *tao* way of life
without force it occurs naturally
and is called ceaseless and faithful
it is known as the law of mundane transposition
in this state you will see yourself as you truly are
this perspective must shock you a little
or it will not be genuine as a picture of your true self

understanding this law of mundane transposition
begets tolerance of self and others

understanding tolerance of self and others
begets wisdom of self and others

understanding the wisdom of self and others
begets infinite insight into self and others

employing the insight of self and others creates resonance with
the heavens
the earth
and man

employing this resonance
creates an alignment with the *tao* way of life

thus aligned you will directly communicate with the miracle
and even in ordinary death will forever be a part of it

CHAPTER SEVENTEEN

this is a warning

beware the constraints of looking
and ceasing to see

the seeds of chaos that were sown

by the sons and daughters
of the emperors and empresses

are buried in the soil
where they can do no harm to your essential nature

you must protect the ancestral treasures
your lifeforce
your essence
your spirit

benevolent altruism
honest authority
observed ceremony
the songs of creativity

can not be managed
by any manner of collective intent

to govern through the *tao* way of life
is to do so without notice
and remain invisible to the world

to govern by the *tao* way of life
granting light and sound to the eyes and ears
attracts the heartmind and heart spirit of the world

to govern through light and sound
without the *tao* way of life
engenders the fear of the world

to govern by unwise force
alone
breeds hatred in the world that nourishes the seeds of chaos

having faith in the faithless
destroys the heart of man
and they become sleeping automatons driven by words and labels
and words as drugs

the method of the true self as original nature
is all that is needed
to embody
to accomplish
wonders

CHAPTER EIGHTEEN

for the decline of the *tao* way of life
begins with prisons of the bodymind
and externally applied rules of the bodymind

defined allegiance
justice blind
equity bound in invisible knots

when judicious thought is the goal
and not thinking
intelligence leads to observed contrast
supplanting the thinking moment

faithless ceremonies are created
that disturb the bodymind

the bodymind is a family
harmonious when

open absence
blends with
full presence

serene when

full presence
blends effortlessly with
will, thought, and imagination

a natural coalescence

will, thought, and imagination
meet and support
the lifeforce

this simple assemblage
speaking directly to the heart spirit
results in a myriad of actions
filled with spontaneity and naturalness

composed and at rest
this family
playing in a field of spontaneous interaction
enjoys peaceful congress with
the shape and void

when the bodymind
is forced
and ill at ease

insincere devotion
to the bodymind
manifests itself
and spills over to every facet of life

rejection of the *tao* way of life
can be checked only through compassion
for the self
for others

then reclamation of the original nature of mankind
can begin

the ancient child asks me to enumerate the steps

the open absence of the bodymind
must combine and share with
the closed presence of the bodymind

the closed presence of the bodymind
must combine and share with
the mind intent of the bodymind

the mind intent of the bodymind
must combine and share with
the lifeforce of the bodymind

the lifeforce of the bodymind
must combine and share with
the heart spirit of the bodymind

the heart spirit of the bodymind
must combine and share with
the spontaneous actions of the bodymind

the spontaneous actions of the bodymind
must combine and share with
the shape and the void

CHAPTER NINETEEN

absolve yourself of the need or desire to be wise and sophisticated
cast off reliance on the frozen thought forms and constructs
that support domesticated behavior
and all life that you meet will benefit exponentially

give up
sham beneficence
false order
civilized equity
and enjoy the true fallibility of the bodymind

then the inner family and its outward reflection

will be serene and commune
harmoniously

reject the practice of manipulating the flow of living

realize that life will wither
in the harsh light of utility
as it becomes an external thing

to be despoiled
compromised

the miracle can only be grasped
through gentle permission given

to oneself

but this alone will not complete the approach

innocent and simple steps must be taken
to reclaim your original nature
these steps must be artless and unadorned

turn inward
search the bodymind

for the unspoiled canvas
upon which your life is painted

with open hands and arms
absorb the powerful simplicity
of your own self
in its lost and genuine embrace

restrain the prejudiced
and narcissistic self
turning outward
to glimpse within

regulate unrestrained need and desire
by extending the plain self
into the moments
created by looking and not seeing

indulging in insecure thoughts and worry for their own sake
exhausts your connection to life's energy and flow

CHAPTER TWENTY

is there any difference
in saying
yes
loudly and with force
and saying
yes
softly with smiling eyes

between those words

whispers weighed
whispered whole

resides the same smoothed hub of assent
that is
my heart

who are you
I am the ancient child

what some say is
good
magnificent
correct

others will say is
bad
decadent
flawed

know that
I refuse
this stultifying jest

and say that
each day which is
a beginning for you
is an end for another

but to me
at least
a thing cannot be correct

if indeed
it is not flawed

am I to be compelled
by false evidence
and looming reality

when that which men truly fear
is merely
themselves seen in each other

the next step is natural
pervasive
take and put comfort in your soul

bodyminds at ease playing in the fires of sacrifice and growth

singing of success and good fortune
brings nourishment to the wanderer
yourself
as new growth in the spring

I pretend that I am floating
solemnly and alone
engineering quietude
allowing tranquillity

my thoughts as grains of sand
released from the hand of my mind
to fall
alone and restful
each thought finding its own place
of stillness

I must form a balance between the world of man about me
and the world of man inside of me

if they gather
then I am alone

if they are abundant
then I am desolate

if they are bereft
then I bring them together in joy

if the white thought is exhausted
then I bring them self-assurance

patiently I move
seeking rest for each moment in space and time
conforming to the gifts of the moment
like the water to the shoreline
helping the families
within and without
to join purposes and grasp and listen and comprehend

I stand alone

for even in a crowd
my simple way is innocently direct and elemental and unique
by that I am singular
rendered aimless and complete
as I absorb the earth's yellow center and lifeforce

CHAPTER TWENTY-ONE

courage
integrity
intellect
mind
respect

all these names
and honored upright human character
are the strengths that flow from the *tao* way of life
emerging from a mystic pass
invisible
as an ever-elusive source

for the *tao* source of living has no shape or form
that can be perceived in ordinary waking consciousness
it is the invisible center of all shapes
the marrow of all forms and hidden quintessence

the present and the past conspire
to hide the name and secret from you

stomp your heels to reveal the conspiracy
as points of fire rise in the blackness of ages past

the inner sense of this mystery gives you comfort
and has always been felt by man
but vital nourishment comes only when you chew on the *tao* way of
life

externalized shapes beyond the apparent confines as manifested
forms
behave as a paternal fool entertaining time itself

by touching the earth beneath your feet
you solidify the moment and know the name

of quintessence unrevealed

CHAPTER TWENTY-TWO

bend the waist	as pliable yellow gold
flex the joints	in the shape of metal
twist the limbs	as a tree

integral growth

make yourself an empty vessel
and receive the lifeforce of the universal

see yourself as deep and vast
yet softly muted to the ordinary world

standing alone under the sky
this firmament over your accepted perceptions

is perpetual renewal in which the smallest piece of wealth

is a vast natural fortune
unnoticed
unless the heavens are above your head

this message is so utterly simple
that it is easily confused by over-thinking

when heaven is in your head
rather than above it
you will be scattered into space
without a home

but when heaven is in its place in the sky
real comprehension and
conscious comprehension
remain fixed to the core center in balance

then
you have returned home

an insightful person embraces and holds the absolute
singularity reflected as the original mind
consuming the consummate

and becomes a limitless model
of plenary usage

containing all the possibilities
of all that is possible

remain esoteric and invite wisdom
deny light to ordinary eyes
and sound to ordinary ears

in order to balance the mind and clear perception

though this ongoing quest is a personal endeavor
refrain from forcing life to be about yourself

do not force the hearts and spirits of others
in self-gratification
for this damages your vitality and essence

denial of accolades from yourself and others
to yourself
is a way to balance the conscious ordinary comprehension
with real comprehension

in this way the ordinary world
will be at peace with you
and you with it

all of this requires you to remain adaptable
to the ever-changing present

| bend | flex | twist |
| pliable gold | shaping metal | living tree |

yes
surely these are watchwords

that preserve the integral gifts of human existence

in that
they belong to all

CHAPTER TWENTY-THREE

indulged fascination of thoughts
your own
revealed as words of one
disturb the fabric
disturb the gifts
of these singular moments
of quintessence revealed

for speech is a blessing if managed
to yourself and others

the same speech is a curse if not managed
to yourself and others

words that intrude will damage essence and vitality

the core of both the speaker and the witness
will be harmed when the event is filled

not-intruding is the natural way of optimistic *tao* nature
for *tao* nature *tao* speaks not in *tao* words

having no-thing to say
it can say everything

and does

expressive *tao* nature rises in a continuous stream that moves
across the land
but it must exhaust itself as part of the natural order
and give support and rest to the receptive side of existence
for everything has its own time, place, and duration

yet all of the lifeforce that manifests in our experience
comes from an earth
with heaven standing at its center

as we stand in the middle of it
it is best that we acquiesce to the truth of it
as well as the truth of our own humanity

holding life in this manner reveals the simplicity of the best
approach

pattern your way of living after the *tao* source of life and you will
begin to perceive it
and it will shape you accordingly

guide your life with the strength and character of the *tao* source of
life
and it will be directed accordingly

but allow confusion into your life and you will be disassociated
accordingly

proper alignment with the *tao* way of life
begets resonance with the *tao* source of life

proper alignment with the strength and character of the *tao* source of
life
begets resonance with the character of the *tao* way of life

alignment with confusion begets dissonance with both the path and
its characteristics
it is at this point you will be separated from the middle position
you will be lost between heaven and earth

Chapter Twenty-four

if you become lost between heaven and earth

you will have no root
you will have no core
you will have no motive force
you will have no lifeforce to extend into living

you will not be luminous
you will not be able to ingest life
you will not be able to think properly
you will not be able to see clearly

showing yourself off
seeing yourself as always correct
passing off information as knowledge
forcing your ideas on others
disturbing the peace of another person's home

these are all symptoms of a cancerous existence
in which your heart spirit is not straight
it is like an arrow shot into the sky
and lost forever

these are distortions and misrepresentations of the virtuous truth of
the *tao* way of life
these are distortions and misrepresentations of the virtuous reasons
for living the *tao* way of life

they are repugnant to us all
so we avoid them

Chapter Twenty-five

the ancient child asks
what is it that is beyond opposites and extremes

to stand upright amid the *tao* source of life

the ancient child asks
how does one do this

stand upright and alone
amidst the chaotic commerce
reveal the mysterious channel of unlimited capacity
with neutral will and intention

distant mind   ever surprised
distant thought   ever alert
distant traveler ever aware

feel the opened space that
exists before and between
heaven and earth

be spontaneously silent, quiet, still, and dynamic
to gain admittance

be naturally isolated, random, genuine, and perennial
to fuse with the changing changelessness and space
that is your ever-present womb, home, and companion

from this place
you stand
for this space is the door and source
from which existence flows
and makes itself known to you

though invisible to me and unnamed
I sense its presence
by its shadow and tracks as it moves through me
and I through it

it is a private experience
intimate in the extreme and latent in antithesis

so I call it the *tao* way of life even as my words evaporate

domesticated people can not perceive its real name
for its name is a word enfolding
miraculous power
stalwart power
constant power
great power

the great is sufficient in itself
for addressing
that which is so close
yet
so far away

that which is separated
yet
intensely unified

that which comes closer to you
as it moves further away

in this greatness the *tao* source of life turns on
the whim of intention
yet
is affected by nothing
sufficient unto itself and its reflections

the *tao* source of life is great from above
heaven as creation is great
earth as receptive is great
man in his humanity is great

tao source of life
heaven as creation
earth as receptive
man in his humanity

all are great
and that's all we can normally see
and we are part of it
as it is part of us

man in his humanity is guided by the receptive earth

receptive earth is guided by heaven as creation

heaven as creation is guided by the *tao* source of life

the *tao* source of life is wrapped in the self-formed gossamer of
spontaneous force
that exists of its own accord

CHAPTER TWENTY-SIX

the ancient child asks
but where can you find the connection

it is a bright moment that can not be grasped

gravity intelligence must have an earth center
to find its core
and bring auspicious stability
to those quarters shallow
and not yet complete

as foundation and embodied root
gravity intelligence
secures profundity in the unprofound

for the planet on which we stand
and its wonders all around us
are both our model and our entry point
to the concentration of impervious integrity

the wise traveler
as gentle soul
is a man reserved and understated
who moves over the land cheerfully

carrying the weight of his own existence
as a cherished memory forever near

only softly at rest and true repose
can he visit the honest gravity intelligence

of his own existence
and rejuvenate himself
for journeys anew

but what motivates someone to retain a sense of humor
about themselves
while showing true concern for the hearts, minds, and lives
of people they have never met

the only answer is the selfsame gravity intelligence

if you have a firm root and core
born of its honest weight
then you will not lose your foundation
life's movement will then be deliberate and unhurried
and will
itself
protect you

CHAPTER TWENTY-SEVEN

the ancient child asks
how should you walk

I should walk as if each step
is touched by nature
and does not disturb the *tao* way of living

the ancient child asks
how should you talk

I should speak with a quiet honesty
that issues from my core
like an inverted bell
and not disturb the peace of others

the ancient child asks
how should you see

I should observe the count of life with my intuition
that honors my memory by setting it free
and not rely on the rational order of things, objects, and quantities

the ancient child asks
how should you enter doorways to infinity

I should regard every threshold as an entrance to a domain
that protects my sense of wonder
and guarantees a stranger's rest in a friendly land

the ancient child asks
how should you join with life

I should bind myself to life with invisible knots
that can not be untied by any man
and I should be forever bound
and forever free

the ancient child asks
should you disregard or reject people

no
I should bless everyone that I meet
and give them a gift
even if only an earth-searching smile

the ancient child asks
should you disregard or reject beneficial goods

no
for everything is useful as a reflection of the *tao* source of life
and if I am not blinded by utility
then I will instantly know how best to employ these goods

the ancient child asks
if you follow this course
who will you be able to help

everyone

the ancient child asks
if you follow this course
who will you be able to teach

everyone

they will provide me with the tools and substance needed to help
and teach them

the ancient child asks
if they already have the tools and substance
why can't they help themselves

because like the emperors and empresses of mankind
they have looked
and ceased to see

having become enamored of looking and not seeing
they require a clever person
to pierce and steal the confusion
and show them the lustrous gossamer road
back to their essential nature

the ancient child asks
is this journey back to their essential nature
a journey to a far away place

no
the essential nature of man is all-pervasive

know the outflowing of lifeforce
from the three places and
strive to be the expressive quality
of the receptive earth
honoring its potential to be filled
with an understated quality of everyday life
and you will return to your essential nature

in this *tao* way of living
you will reclaim your innocence

Chapter Twenty-nine

the ancient child asks
can you control the universe by overtly grasping it
can you shape and bend it to your will with outward force
can you assert yourself over nature and truly control it

no
the uncreated can be grasped only by not grasping it
the uncreated can be willed only by an inward force
the uncreated can be controlled only by releasing control
completely

yes
control by surrendering
bend and shape through an inward willing
passively assert through active non-assertion

to make it is to spoil it
to hold it is to lose it

the ancient child asks
should you interfere with the world

no
to interfere with the world puts it just outside your reach
you can not succeed
the unfolding world is a heavenly vessel which can not be made
because it already exists
beyond desire and conception
and always has

attempting to create it
scars it
sometimes beyond recognition

to make it is to spoil it
to hold it is to lose it

do not interfere
dance with it instead

some things go forward
other things recede
some things lead
other things follow
some things blow hot
other things blow cold
some are strong
others are weak
some things are separate
other things come together
some things stand
other things fall

CHAPTER THIRTY

the ancient child asks
who can help

anyone

the ancient child asks
who can help you

everyone

the ancient child asks
how can you help them

by showing them how to be resolute

the ancient child asks
how can they help you

by learning to be resolute

the ancient child asks
what is resolute

not violent
not arrogant
not boastful
not haughty
not weak
not obsequious

the ancient child asks
why must they be resolute

because there is no other way to enter the *tao* source of life

the ancient child asks
who acts with resolve and determination

a good man
who protects his essential nature and abhors unwise force
but acts when it is time to act
acts resolutely
stops and withdraws

the ancient child asks
violence
is it resolute

no

the ancient child asks
is it just

no

the ancient child asks
if I project violence outward what will happen

it comes back to me

the ancient child asks
can a violent man be fine-spun

no

the ancient child asks
can a violent man find the *tao*

no

the ancient child asks
who made this sword

a man

the ancient child asks
was the man who made this sword fine-spun

yes
if it is a good sword
yes

fine-spun man
fine-spun sword
together they ride the winds
move the heavens
and rule the earth

the ancient child asks
how do they do this

it is a secret held in your hands

the ancient child asks
when is this secret revealed

only when it is necessary

if the secret is revealed too soon it is spoiled and despised
then the sword and the man are of no use to themselves or others

the ancient child asks
where does wisdom come from

I hear it in my left ear
it floats

the ancient child asks
where does anger come from

I hear it in my right ear
it falls hard

the ancient child asks
which is fine-spun

the left

the ancient child asks
can you force wisdom to speak to your left ear

no
it speaks when it is ready
you have to wait
the right speaks all the time
it is deafening

the ancient child asks
how can you stop the right from speaking all the time

by gently
lying down
sitting
standing and
walking

the ancient child asks
where does this work best for you

at my home where things are familiar and I feel safe
anger can be stopped there with the four virtues

home is anywhere I can feel the *tao* beneath my feet
my feet must be fine-spun as well

the ancient child asks
what do your fine-spun feet tell you

do not find joy in hurting people
if you must hurt someone
listen to the left
keep your heart spirit calm
and be fine-spun
you can not find the *tao* source of life if you enjoy being violent
and hurt people, their land, and even their animals on the land
if you live life violently
the life around you will disappear

there is a time to be happy and a time to be sad
know how to differentiate between the two so you know where to
lie

sit
stand
walk
if you cultivate these virtues you will be happy
if someone is hurt be sad
treat it like a funeral
because an opportunity to enter the *tao* has died

CHAPTER THIRTY-TWO

the *tao* source of life is vast and unlimited
the *tao* source of life is beyond ordinary reason and logic
the *tao* source of life is unfathomable and unnamable
it is beyond words and labels
it is beyond deliberateness

the ancient child asks
why can't you grasp it

because it's too big and too small at the same time
because it is one thing and many things at the same instant
and you can not divide it into parts
it can not be held or known on purpose

utility is useful for only a short time

these are instructions

lie down
sit
stand
walk in a deliberate manner
allow heaven into your bodymind
draw the earth into your bodymind
let them mingle around the center of your bodymind
resisting the desire to command or control
it will feel like a gentle rain is falling within and without you
swallow the saliva like it was honey
that condenses like a sweet dew into your core
and rest peacefully and naturally within the *tao* source of life
knowing that its heartbeat
is your own

the heartbeat will shape, carve, and form you into what is needed
at this moment in space and time and no more

do not be in a hurry for the future
rather allow the unnamed to flow into the named to reveal the
present ever

embodying balance, poise, and equilibrium
you will have no difficulty seeing
you are a part of a vast undifferentiated whole
you are a swirling eddy in the great river
you are a drop of water in the great ocean

despite what your dividing mind says
remind yourself
that you are always home

CHAPTER THIRTY-THREE

focus and forget

learn to understand the outside world by looking inward
and you will access true and authentic wisdom
learn to understand the inside world by looking outward
and you will access true and authentic knowledge

when true and authentic wisdom and true and authentic knowledge
intermingle, you will see
wise force at work and know how to employ it

control the useful parts with it
control the border between the inside world and the outside world
with it

be aware, alert, and relaxed as you are the crux of the moment

the *tao* will take you by surprise
flame, light, fog, and cloud appear
as boundaries are dissolved
and senses burned away

employ wise force to manage the moment
deliver confusion to the earth
rest comfortably
weep if you must but only in joyousness
and you will secure a silent and gentle victory

the *tao* source of life reaches out for you as you reach out for it
effortlessly flow into one another
feel the divine force spinning and oscillating to and from every
quarter
and be content to know that
the plan upon which all of the universe is built
is perfect and complete
benevolent and giving

we have all that we require

protect the moment with the will, thought, and imagination
project yourself boldly in space and time
as you fortify all that has preceded it

remember where you are

remember where you came from

remember your significance as a facet of the *tao* source of life

you are everlasting

you can not die within the *tao* source of life

CHAPTER THIRTY-FOUR

the ancient child asks
how does it feel

the great *tao* source of life floats and drifts
it is a candle in a room filled with mirrors
it is a diamond in a room filled with candles and mirrors

the great *tao* source of life flows and undulates
it is a spider's web that stretches in every direction
it is wondrously expansive and cyclical and unique

the great *tao* source of life has a rhythm to it
it revolves and spins in every direction
it connects and binds all things with freedom and independence
and interdependence

when you are aware of all these things
a light and sensitive energy collects at your crown
and space and time literally break apart

usual becomes unreality
reality becomes unusual

everything depends on this
it always has
it always will be

name it paint it sing it if you must
but trust it as silence
a blank canvas in the unnamed

it can not die
neither can you

if you remain humble and quiet a new mind will be born
where puzzles are solved in their own space and time
where unique thinking that is greater than thought flows like water
where flowing into human life

transforms human life

then you will be a great sage wise man

Chapter Thirty-five

hold and embody

be the one who will hold and embody the *tao* way of life
by shaping yourself with the great ultimate symbol
by holding yourself within the confluence of its meeting rhythms
be the one who centers themselves between heaven and earth

and move about in the field of unlimited possibilities

you will breathe with your skin
you will shine with every breath

and quicken the way you lay, sit, stand, and walk

this is the true breathing that inspires and attracts true life
this is the true breathing that inspires and attracts the *tao* source of
life

each breath is an illumination
there are many illuminations

the ancient child asks
what follows
what flows in and flows out

sturdy comfort
abundant rest
organized serenity
and a smile

a silent song of the sweetest music
a sweet taste of honey swallowed gently
a desire to play, dance, paint, and sing

I am actually singing in a world that is somehow
bigger
brighter
funnier

more wondrous than I could have possibly imagined
I want to reach out to strangers and passersby
I want to visit with them
I want to talk with them
I want to laugh with them

the ancient child asks
are these ghosts or real people

it doesn't matter

complete the ritual
draw the words in a ghost's sandbox
don't stop until it's time
your guests want you to complete the contract
remember
you stand between heaven and earth
you are the middle place

the ancient child asks
can you feel my hand on your spine

yes I can
my spine is part of a roof that protects me

the ancient child says
yes it is
paint the changes you feel in your spine
show me where life rushes into you
show me where life rushes out

I paint the symbols
heaven, earth, wind, water, mountain, fire, thunder, and lake

the ancient child asks
what do you see

I see a circle of jade

the ancient child asks
what do you hear

I hear a woman singing

the ancient child asks
where are you

I am in a church or a temple

the ancient child asks
what color is the road outside

it is blue-green

the ancient child asks
what are you doing now

I am rocking back and forth
I can not stop
and my hair is tickling me

the ancient child asks
what are your emotions

I feel anxious
your hand is hot on my back

the ancient child says
think of a warm waterfall
focus on your brush and continue to paint

my family is all sitting around a table reading and talking

the ancient child asks
is the table upstairs or downstairs

our dining room is upstairs

the ancient child asks
what do you see

a bowl of fruit in the center

the ancient child asks
where are you

I am on a farm

the ancient child asks
what time of year is it

it is my birthday

these places can not be seen or heard
these places are innumerable and inexhaustible and subtle
you have the power to go to any of these places
if you will but return there often
visit, commune, and rest there
don't speak of them
because words as drugs and words as labels are coarse
they will rob them of their real taste

instead
simply
remember

return home

CHAPTER THIRTY-SIX

the ancient child says
to see the future
put your left hand over your breast bone
and look into your right palm

rotate your fist as if gathering yarn left and right
expand yourself to every quarter
until you feel the orbiting movements of the planets within you

draw an imaginary gossamer bow and shoot an arrow
left and right

the ancient child asks
but what are arrows

arrows are wishes and thought forms

weak at rest
strong in motion

they will find their mark
if the archer is calm, focused and controlled

the ancient child asks
how do you condense your bodymind, spirit, and lifeforce

collect yourself to your core center
by reaching out with your bodymind
in order to go definitely inward
you must definitely reach outward

the ancient child asks
how do you condense your bodymind and spirit and lifeforce

reach out with your bodymind and support the heavens above you
using absolutely no strength at all

keep your five fingers open if you want to grasp silver and gold

the ancient child asks
how can this be
what is the secret

it is a game without a winner
you are both contestants
it is a joyous dance
you are both dancers
it is a puppet show
you are the marionette and the hands manipulating strings

each of us is subtle and hidden away
revealed only by the true breath

out reaching
out shining

both are allowed to happen because
the *tao* way of life can never be forced
it can only be invited in

the voice of the wonderwork is subtle and hidden away
you must be quiet and still to hear it clearly
the light of the wonderwork is subtle and hidden away
you must move about mysteriously and make tiny adjustments in
your bodymind to see it clearly
the substance of the wonderwork is subtle and hidden away
you must touch and caress it by letting it touch and caress you

the taste of the wonderwork is subtle and hidden away
you must turn your tongue in an empty mouth to savor it

the aroma of the wonderwork is subtle and hidden away
you must rely on afterthoughts, memories, and musings to reveal its
smell

silent victory
quietly conquering

this is how you should behave

that is the secret

the ancient child asks
can you not see it clearly
are you a fish stubbornly dying on the dry shore
refusing to enter the ocean
until you understand it clearly

the ancient child asks
is there anything to be gained by killing yourself

there is nothing to be gained by suicide

the ancient child says
use the natural gifts you have to explore
your inner world

after all
it's a sin to ignore your talents

do you think that your talents are for showing off

CHAPTER THIRTY-SEVEN

the *tao* source of life as a
ceaseless and everlasting universal force
is oblique

and never does any single thing
yet always does every single thing

hold this idea firmly in your mind
and your body will naturally align
with the universal force

senses and consciousness will turn inward
and your whole being will rest peacefully
while
your pure and elegant nature spontaneously
fills you up
denying purchase to all confusion and unnaturalness

this is how you transform yourself
by anchoring yourself amidst the flow
of a sea of life force

by tranquilly sitting between
heaven and earth

by turning around and listening
to your soul

CHAPTER THIRTY-EIGHT

the ancient child asks
how do you turn around and listen to your soul

by selflessly acting with
the power of authentic benevolence

you can not plan to do good works
good works can only be done naturally

a person who plans to be good
will have no power
and will not be authentic

the difference between authentic and inauthentic
is the benevolent power of your soul

an authentic man never acts
an authentic man has no hidden agenda
an authentic man seeks no rewards for his deeds

an inauthentic man tries too hard
an inauthentic man has ulterior motives
an inauthentic man constantly thinks of rewards

authenticity can not be willed or proscribed
authenticity can not be planned or enforced

false manners are a sham

morality worn like a coat gives rise to shallowness
that casts a shadow
over everyone

rules and propriety arise from this darkness
constricting the hearts and minds of humanity
forcing their souls
to a hiding place

life becomes chaotic

great men lecture you on your faults
complicating simple things
until
they are barely recognizable

and you don't know which way to turn

but the authentic man
allows his soul to take the lead of his life
holds firmly to his inner truth
gently grasping the seed of life

CHAPTER THIRTY-NINE

authenticity
who are you
where do you reside
what sustains you
where do you go

I am the original bodymind
I live in the folds of essence, energy, and spirit
the *tao* way of life sustains me

I move about in the vast undifferentiated realm
and the field of all that is possible

inhale and make the sound
exhale and make the sound
and write

life	live	grow
full	abundance	fulfillment
divine	potent	spiritual
rest	repose	serene
pure	clear	water

since ancient times these have been the keys
living and growing to an abundance of spiritual force and
energized serenity acquired through tranquility

the pivot is a bowl of water left alone and undisturbed
so the surface becomes as clear as glass
able to reflect

illumination
balance, poise, and equilibrium

these are the secrets of wholeness
within the *tao* way of life

without the *tao* way of life
heaven, earth, and man are divided

life
fullness
divinity
tranquility
clarity

would all be forfeit

Chapter Forty

the first step is to enter the place
from whence you came

the second step is to play in the field of limitlessness

the third step is to demonstrate birth, growth, maturation, and
death

the fourth step is to rest quietly
listening for wisdom and the sacred sounds
watching the web of moving existence all around you

rest
and then

play again

CHAPTER FORTY-ONE

the very best students of the *tao* way of life
try their best to be open to its mysteries
by using their higher intuition and naturally entering its
transcendental shape

they simply look
they simply see

the typical students of the *tao* way of life
try their best to let the mysteries in
but get in their own way by thinking into it too much

they look halfheartedly
they can not see clearly

those students of the *tao* way of life that are worthless
can not be said to really be students at all
because they can not sense, see, or reason
when they hear about the mysteries

they laugh, ridicule, and demean the whole idea

what they do not realize
is that they are only seeing
their own blindness

what they do not know
is that laughter
is the taoist way of seeing

laughter outlines the great mystery

the ancient child asks
what are the first qualities of a student of the *tao* way of life

higher intuition and the ability to laugh with a full heart

if you can not laugh
you can not know the *tao* way of life

a wisdom thread that stretches back to antiquity tells us
what is real and true and how to recognize it

the bright path seems dim
cloudy

the direct path seems crooked
obscured

the smooth and level path
actually bobs and weaves

true strength of character seems weak to the ignorant
authentic white always carries a part of blackness with it

true abundance is actually empty

can you see it

the greatest stability is actually tenuous

can you feel it

the highest certitude is actually a lie

can you find truth that easily

the transcendental shape has no walls or limit

can you move into it

the transcendental shape is small and unfillable

can you fill it up

the greatest talent requires time and work to ripen
can you patiently wait for it

practice does not make perfect
practice is perfect to begin with

can you really behave that way

the greatest sound is actually silent

can you hear it

living the *tao* way of life is so ancient and natural
that it has no name
it is so accessible and pervasive
that you can not see it
yet it is both the beginning and the end of everything
that lends its profound magic to the entire world

CHAPTER FORTY-TWO

living the *tao* way of life creates resonance
and a life that is lived

resonance possessed of its own momentum creates difference
difference possessed of its own momentum creates
heaven
man
earth

the union of these three produces everything in the universe
in a continuous wave
that can be embraced and ridden
by obliquely drifting within it

the ancient child asks
how can you drift with the universal

by precisely blending my bodymind's lifeforce

the ancient child asks
what must be blended to drift with the universal

body must blend with mind
mind must blend with will
will must blend with lifeforce
lifeforce must blend with spirit
spirit must blend with engaged movement
engaged movement must blend with the void

the void is a doorway that sits at the center
of the universe

the ancient child asks
where is the doorway

between the beats of my heart
between the inbreath and the outbreath
between the beats of a drum

between the decision and the initiation
between my intention and my action
between the words on this page

drift and fly
by standing still
feeling the continuity
of the universe

there is nothing to worry about
no matter where life takes you
you are not alone and
you never have been

sometimes drift more and sometimes less
sometimes stop and look around
sometimes briskly fly from peak to peak

an authentic journey can not be forced

it unfolds with jostles and bumps
it sways to and fro

this is the only way to live

CHAPTER FORTY-THREE

the most soft and ethereal things of the world
will always easily penetrate the hard and unyielding

those things that are without form
will always penetrate the impervious structure

because the true heart of hardness is
soft

because the true heart of impervious solidity is
formlessness

the artist can not paint a picture of water without
showing its source or
showing its destination

water will always wear down a stone

when I see water naturally seeking its own resting place
I know that it will arrive at that point
no matter what gets placed in the way

flow naturally like water
without contention or coercion
and you will arrive at your destination
and resting place

few understand the wisdom of unforced non-action
because it can not be expressed with words and labels
it can only be intuitively felt

it can only be understood with the softness and formlessness
of water

it can only be implemented with the softness and formlessness
of water

Chapter Forty-four

what is more important to you
what others think of you or
what you think of your body, mind, and spirit

is your natural energy, essence, and inspiration
worth more to you than acquired material things

is gaining
more or less
painful than losing

speaking with the mystery
refining your nature
studying your emotions
will inform you

if you love well
you will spend yourself well

if you love too often
you will exhaust yourself and die

when the power of the *tao* source of life
flows into you from above
contentment and happiness abound

when you know how to extend your love and life
in a way that does not impose itself on the universe
then you will flow into it
knowing when to move forward and backward
when to twist left or right
when it's time to float upward or settle downward
when it's best to move on
or simply stand still

know these things and you will realize your limitlessness

be the sacred friend that joins the hands
of heaven and earth
accepting all the flaws and faults
within and without your bodymind
bearing on your shoulders
the good and the bad all around you

and you will preserve the bodymind of the world

CHAPTER FORTY-FIVE

sit quietly

focus and forget

rest within the great achievement

the ancient child asks
what is the great achievement

it is beyond description in any language
it can only be felt intuitively
it can only be expressed intuitively
engage a loose, alert, and aware
body, mind, and sound
then look into the formless
and perceive no thing

see yourself as a sphere
small at first
growing to encompass
the vastness of infinite space

sit quietly
focus and forget then
in a state of ease and rest
secure the truth of the great achievement

employing the truth will not exhaust its power
when it seems exhausted it is really abundant
and while human art will die at the hands of utility
the great achievement is beyond being useful

great straightness is curved and crooked
great intelligence is raw and silly
great words are simple and naturally awkward

engaged movement drives out the frozen cold
mindful stillness subdues the frenzied heart

sit quietly
focusing
forgetting
summon order from the void
that guides the ordering of the universe

CHAPTER FORTY-SIX

when the powers and strengths of heaven
float downward into the earth
through man
the *tao* way of life presents itself
to everyone and everything

horses trained by men behave naturally and spontaneously
without any need for direction or control
their beneficence unfolds naturally

but when the powers and strengths of heaven
are blocked from flowing into the earth
man becomes isolated
and inoffensive creatures become warlike
multiplying in great numbers
and profaning the sacred
as the *tao* way of life recedes

the ancient child asks
what then presents itself

dissatisfaction with one's own essential nature
dissatisfaction with one's own gifts and deficits
dissatisfaction with the very ground one stands on

the worst thing you can do is to
extend and reach into the world
from a place of scarcity instead of abundance

one is restful
the other is restless

the restless place is an unnatural field
sown with discontentment

the restful place is an inexhaustible sacred precinct
that goes where you go
providing everything you need

in just the right amounts

secure the restful place
stand
allow the power and strength of heaven
to flow downward
through you
to the earth
and quietly watch
the *tao* way of life present itself
to everyone and everything

CHAPTER FORTY-SEVEN

the ancient child asks
what is authentic knowledge

only revealed knowledge is authentic knowledge
it flows from the heart's center
within our way of living

the ancient child asks
what is the heart center within our way of living

at the center of my own heart
wherever I may be

alive

to know the world is not
to think into it by reason

reason is not revelation

to know the world is
to allow the world
to think into you

wherever it may be

authentic knowing is revealed
in a soul and to a soul
seeking its lost home
and resting place
within deep regions
of a centered heart spirit

the mysteries of the world
come to you in a living light
that breathes as you breathe
infused with your own thoughts
yet outlined as some distant place
or thing

you may bring discipline to your knowing
but you can not bend it or shape it
because it is already perfectly formed

you may know the world completely and
understand its workings
without ever leaving home

the ancient child asked
what are the impediments to authentic knowing

wrong error is the first
conquered by quiet sitting

wrong flight is the second
conquered by flying obliquely with ease

wrong meditation is the third
conquered by contemplative ritual

wrong purification is the fourth
conquered by openness within a sacred precinct

wrongly embracing the doubt and despair of others as they are
conquered by a humble appreciation of yourself as you are

the *tao* way of life bestows knowledge
of all things under heaven
to those who can travel the entire world
with one ordinary deliberate step

in a lush green forest

one step

CHAPTER FORTY-EIGHT

this one ordinary deliberate step

takes you away from increase
takes you away from scholarship
takes you away from the material intellect

and makes you a relaxed wanderer
who knows more and more
by knowing less and less

the usual is used and loses
the unusual is experienced and gains

the world yields readily to suggestion

by swinging your bodymind open like a gate
you allow the world to enter
at the behest of your intention

enjoy the wonderwork
as your invited guests mingle within
fill their glasses
arrange introductions
and allow the moment to unfold
without any interference or commentary

wherever you wander

be the perfect host
be happy to be there

CHAPTER FORTY-NINE

a wise man does not think first and then act
when the *tao* way of life presents itself

thinking first stops the moment from unfolding

when a mystery appears
he experiences it as completely as he is able
drawing no conclusions about it

when his heart and mind are uplifted
he feels
that dreams are far more tangible
than waking truths

he treats every one and every thing
with equanimity

he declares
I hold the good and able
as good and able

I hold the bad and inept
as good and able

to hold them all
as equal and excellent
is to gain virtue
exponentially

for one person or thing
is not
more or less
important
than any other
person or thing

truth is truth
lies are truth

experiencing life in this way
trains the bodymind
to be united
with the virtuous way of experiencing life

you become peaceful and reserved
drifting
within the field of all possibilities

playing like a child

CHAPTER FIFTY

when the energy of heaven
meets the energy of earth
birth and death appear

between birth and death
life appears

my bodymind opens to life
nine ways
my bodymind moves through life
with four limbs

these thirteen parts together
can move to create life or
can move to create death

those who create death
try to harden their life
against it
by forcing their life
into still suits of armor

those who create life
are impervious
to claws and teeth
to horns and blades
to dangers above and below

the ancient child asks
how can they do this

because they know how to
step deliberately and move
towards the creation of life

Chapter Fifty-one

the *tao* brings forth life
the path and power of virtue nurtures that life

the spine of the world shapes them
the mind of the world moves and completes them
they are of a piece
forming a harmonious unit

that is why a natural reverence
for the *tao* way of life and its power
manifests spontaneously

the *tao* way of life produces everything
the way of virtue nourishes everything through
birth
growth
maturation and
death
and acts as a protector and guide

mystic virtue assists but does not control
as such it is mysterious to everyone
and virtuous to all

the mystic knows
that it is difficult to know
which thoughts of *tao* making
are his
and which thoughts flow
from the interplay
of life and its nurturing

remember

the *tao* way of life
allows

CHAPTER FIFTY-TWO

realizing the interplay of the *tao* way of life
and the virtue of nurturing all things under heaven
will introduce you to the primal mother

the mother of the world

resting peacefully with the mother
will introduce you to her sons and daughters

the sons and daughters of the world

these children can be exhausting
and though they mean no harm
trying to follow or control them
will only bring great danger to you

to be safe
rest peacefully with the mother

gently close your eyes
and look inward

softly direct your ears
to listen within

lightly close your mouth
raise your tongue to its roof
and quietly savor the interior

gently lift your crown
sit firm with a relaxed hold
on your bodymind

and let her love
fill you up

you will never be empty
again

remember
chasing children
brings calamity
no matter
how hard
you try
to follow
or grasp
them

the whole universe is in the palm
of your hand
but without
illumination
you can not see it

the real world is not open
to the rational mind

the ancient child asks
when you have rested sufficiently
in the arms of the primal mother
and your vision begins to clear
what occurs

it is an unexpected sense of making
that first arises within the bodymind

then you are engulfed in a benevolent flame
that outlines rather than burns
and I do not know if I am
the source or the witness

the senses play
leaping to and fro
mischievously acting against their nature

emotions of comfort and satisfaction swell
so that even the harshest rain
feels like a lover's kiss

resting deeper
you feel as if an unseen enemy
has been vanquished
and life courses through your limbs
as the warrior's belt collects you

the connection to the *tao* source and way of life
becomes punctuated and definite
possessed of a wholly benevolent clarity

language leaves you
and a light and sensitive energy collects at your crown

visions cascade upon you so rapidly
that it becomes impossible
to divide or discern
what we normally regard as real

death becomes impossible

fire and force penetrate deeply
within your bodymind
and a new truth shapes you
into someone altogether different

you begin to breathe
the *tao* way of life
as true respiration
within a quickening
that shines out
for all to see

spinning out of the quickening
you understand the mother's children
you sing and dance
you paint and play
you look at the palm of your hand and

you see

you can still make mistakes
you can still be confused
you can still misstep
but you will always have the eyes of the *tao*

however
should you ever see yourself as separate from it

you will cease
to see
altogether

CHAPTER FIFTY-THREE

authentic knowledge is intuitive knowledge
authentic knowledge is directly experienced

it is easy to enter the *tao* source and way of life
through higher intuition

all you have to do is
enter a sacred precinct
pick up your life and bodymind
adjust it to the moment in space and time
play and create in the moment
be happy and content with whatever occurs

revel with your creation
rest with your creation
rejoice with your creation

when timeworn ritual feels new
you will see exactly where you are going
and be able to walk the magnificent path
in freedom measures
slowly and deliberately

it is easy to get sidetracked and lost in the wilderness
it happens all the time
but
the worst thing you can do
is worry too much about it

smile
correct the course
bring yourself back to the great road and walk
slowly and deliberately

nothing else will solve the problem of getting lost

imposed order and rigid ritual are too clean
and won't produce anything of substance or beauty

magic coats with secret symbols can not nullify
anger, violence, or confusion
at the center of a lost man

an authentic life can not be stolen
false spirit is not the *tao* way of life

when order is imposed and ritual defiled
when anger, violence, and confusion are purposefully disguised
when you feed the stomach but not the soul
when you boast, brag, and push yourself on the world

you get further and further away from the *tao* source and way of life
indeed
you are its enemy

CHAPTER FIFTY-FOUR

to be firmly rooted in the *tao* way of life
a bodymind must stand upright
placing a portion of itself beneath the surface
of the planet

standing naturally in this way
enlivens the spirit
preventing confusion and disturbance

the ancient child asks
what are the watchwords for standing rooted in the *tao*

balanced	poised	equilibrium
ease	relaxation	naturalness
loose	playful	embrace

hold these nine and stand

you will not be shaken

your thoughts and their offspring
will become ordered and finely tuned
possessed of an endless clarity
ritualistically conforming to the flux and flow of the seasons

this is authenticity born of higher intuition
resting on the shoulders of one
truly alive

when a person holds the nine
he becomes genuine
influencing his family

when a family holds the nine
they manifest abundance
influencing their town and immediate locality

when a town and immediate locality hold the nine
they are filled with inner strength and wise force
influencing the entire country

when a country holds the nine
it extends its blessings worldwide
cultivating pervasive goodness everywhere

can you see it

a single person standing in the *tao* way of life
brings the life of the *tao* way to the world

for each of you

guided by higher intuition and taoist sight
identify every one you meet as part of your self
identify every thing you meet as part of your self

then you will see deeply
into the truth of your self
as you see deeply into the truth of others

CHAPTER FIFTY-FIVE

vital essence
a hand supporting your back

lifeforce energy
a hand cradling your abdomen

human spirit
a hand touching your heart

when these are balanced, poised, and equal
you become spontaneous and full of life

when they are cultivated with ease, relaxation, and naturalness
you resonate harmonically with the *tao*

when you stay loose and playful reaching out to embrace the world
you become an invincible child impervious to harm

you will see

but if you allow them to compete
with each other
one of them will exhaust the other two
and you will surely die young

what is dying
dying is walking away
from the *tao* way of life

CHAPTER FIFTY-SIX

anyone who really understands the *tao* way of life
finds living it easier than talking about it

anyone who really understands the *tao* way of life
finds that talking about it gets in the way of living it

children become noisy and unruly and they crave attention

requiting dissonance involves diving into the earth
turning your senses inward
protecting your stores
unbinding your bodymind
tempering harsh glare and sharp edges

plunging deeply into the heart of the mystery
generates a wholeness for yourself
that is a wholeness of the world

at that point
the world honors you
because you honor the world

CHAPTER FIFTY-SEVEN

think of yourself as an empire
to govern, explore, work, and live in

a man stretched between heaven and earth
governs the totality of the self
with ritual action and intent

a man stretched between heaven and earth
resolves conflicts within his borders
with surprise, creativity, and the unusual

a man stretched between heaven and earth
embraces the universe
by not interfering with it at all

it is a matter of degree
to see yourself as a ruler who governs
according to a definite plan
reacting creatively to the unexpected
while also
allowing your kingdom to unfold naturally

the ancient child asks
where is this kingdom

the kingdom is within me
within each of us

too many taxes
too many laws
and the kingdom will never be right

make just the precise amount of demands
upon the kingdom of the self
and you will be happy and abundant
righted between heaven and earth

too many taxes
too many laws
and the kingdom will be in chaos
it will act out of scarcity
it will breed many thieves robbing their countrymen
as the populace arms itself for survival
for survival instead of living

the ancient child asks
how do you remedy the situation

do things without appearing to do things
act spontaneously within the limits of the moment
touch the kingdom with a gentle hand
embrace peace and cultivate stillness
shape your intention and let it overflow
allow good things to happen without meddling
allow your bodymind to order itself

cultivate for the sheer joy of cultivation alone

stretch yourself between heaven and earth
mindfully chip away at your life
to see
what is inside

do everything
by
doing nothing

CHAPTER FIFTY-EIGHT

govern yourself with a light and sensitive energy
of hand, heart, and intent
and you will behave as one unified being

govern yourself without a light and sensitive energy
gently holding your heart behind a gate
and you will never be unified
as you pry and intrude upon yourself
becoming a collection of decaying parts

happiness
misery

the seed of one is always within
the other

they both come from heaven
they both fold one on the other
they both hide from each other
they both surprise each other
they both speak to each other
in a private language only they understand

this is the interplay of yin and yang
you can not stop or control it

seeing things as separate brings illusion and calamity

conform and shape yourself
to the interplay of the yin and yang

discipline and order yourself
like a great square without sharp edges or corners

train and integrate yourself in order
to cut through confusion and illusion

without hurting yourself or others

it is difficult to illuminate without blinding

that is why the sage wise man strives for the authentic
and not the artificial

Chapter Fifty-nine

if you want to bring
order, peace, and prosperity
to yourself
then use a light hand and be gentle
with yourself

establish a routine and stick to it
step through the nine palaces
patterning yourself after nature

cultivate in the early morning hours
stand like a tree
accumulating power, strength, and virtue

master all your treasures under the heavens
sit like a mountain
purifying your mind and consciousness

fortify your talents
recline like a great river
flowing throughout the land, towns, and countryside

collect your knowledge and wisdom
crawl on your hands and knees
penetrating deeply into the earth
awakening to your own endurance and potential
learn to appreciate your limits and you will be unlimited

release yourself to the *tao* way of life
roll firmly within the great mystery
absorbing the everlasting nourishment of living

create and play
become clairsentient
to the *tao* source of life
and you will become a boundless and everlasting immortal

CHAPTER SIXTY

it is important that you attend to great matters
as if they were small and delicate ones
or your inner and outer worlds will be uneasy
and confused

hands on
hands off

a nourishing meal requires
just enough presentation
and not
one bit
more

when the influence of the *tao* source of life
exists itself through many cultivators
across the land
evil has less impact or potential

the ancient child asks
how is this possible

because a sage wise man evenly stretched
between heaven and earth
coaxes his soul from within and
allows it to take the lead
in his life

no ghost
demons or
tormentors
can hurt him
inner or outer

soon his balanced benevolence overflows
to everyone and everything
around him

and the influence of the *tao* source of life
envelopes and protects the world under heaven
allowing its original nature
to present itself

CHAPTER SIXTY-ONE

here is the formula
for discovery
of the original self

see yourself as a great river
identify with the fountainhead in the mountains
identify with the watercourse across the land
identify with the emptying into the great sea

this is the receptive

rest peacefully within the shape of
an empty vessel
blanketing your bodymind with stillness

tranquil sitting
balances the naturally expressive
with the naturally receptive

see the great river within you
see the great river beneath you
see the great river above you
see yourself as small within the great river

the great and the small have no meaning
on their own
because they are the same thing

they wish to serve each other

bring them together
as the river connects the mountain spring
to the vast ocean

and the original self
will appear

CHAPTER SIXTY-TWO

manifesting the *tao* way of life
requires you to emulate the great river
under the heavens

and flow with the watercourse of seasons

surrendering to the natural ordering
brings you to the repository
of all knowledge and wisdom
that only the original mind
can see
or use

magic words will not gain you entrance
good deeds will only shape your intention
but will still not let you in

open your back and front
open the waist
open the arms and legs

play freely without judging
your gifts and your deficits
for your entire being
is a treasure

stretch upward with your crown
and see yourself
sitting peacefully and ordered

within the three
golden elixir fields of cinnabar
in their peaceful order

hold your heart gently
for it is a round jade disc
with a hole in the center

presented to the task at hand
as a great gift
offered to the *tao* source of life

move your arms and legs
restrained at the cliff
demonstrating your nobility, power, and inner strength

hold your symbol of the *tao* source of life
high above your head
as if holding a hammer that will never fall

and the vast and mysterious repository
will open and flow
into you

Chapter Sixty-Three

act decisively by actively
being still and appearing
to do no thing

hear what others will not hear
taste what others will not taste
touch what others will not touch
smell what others will not smell
feel what others will not feel
think what others will not think

reach into the small and make it large
touch the multitudes and with a turn of your wrist
make them few

know the virtue of turning your palm
from covering the earth
to supporting the heavens
and those things that are wrong within and without
will be righted

attend the moment
at the moment
do not wait until the task is half over

being one degree askew in the beginning
results in missing your destination altogether
and no matter how well planned a journey is
there will always be a need for course corrections

in fact
sage wise men will not even think about a destination

before their journey
begins
they have already
arrived

if you make a promise to yourself
keep it

not going to your heart spirit
forces it to come to you
in disorder
that disturbs the bodymind
crippling it to living

approach everything with respect for the magic
inside of it
adhering to the terms of each encounter
so life will unfold
easily

Chapter Sixty-four

that which is

balanced   poised   equal   .

will be peaceful and at rest
amidst the flow

the key is your spirit and its management

the ancient child asks
how do you manage your spirit

embrace active non-action effortlessly
balance yin and yang within your bodymind
poise your will, thought, and imagination
equalize your lifeforce and be under its influence
believe in yourself but never compete
wear your spirit like a radiant mantle
surrender to the deep pleasure of individual attention

remember
building nine palaces can begin
with a single earthen brick
held in your hand
if you give it your undivided attention

ten is real
ten times ten is genuine
ten times ten times ten is pure

steps taken in an authentic journey
possessed of breadth and depth
must rise up from the earth
to meet your feet
which take each step as if it were
the first
and only
step
you will ever take

never try
only do

and then
use your spirit to communicate

project the pleasurable depth of your spirit
outward
extending authenticity and simple pride
to all

experience your self as intimately connected
to all
awakening a unified bodymind response
at just the right moment
in space and time

it is much easier for the *tao* to believe in you
if you believe in yourself

CHAPTER SIXTY-FIVE

men of excellent virtue during ancient times
were very skilled in cultivating
the *tao* way of life
but knew the dangers of understanding
something
too quickly

unsophisticated people will speculate
beyond what they intrinsically know
and draw conclusions
false and firm

combating the false and firm
requires humor and astonishment

it becomes difficult to harmonize the bodymind
when you think
that you know it all

cleverness traps the bodymind
certitude robs the bodymind

outer knowledge
must reconcile with
inner knowledge

those who understand these two
allow distance to measure itself
instead of measuring distance
because directly experiencing
mystic virtue
requires turning inward and reconciling
your inner life
with
your outer life

harmonizing the seen with the unseen

CHAPTER SIXTY-SIX

the ancient child asks
how do you access this great harmony

by becoming a long river flowing downward into the sea
of consciousness, mind, and will
seeking the lowly resting point
slowly along the way
not compressed by earthen dams
but naturally guided to the sea

the ancient child asks
how should you stand and speak to the world around you

with a portion of myself
within the earth
as nourishing root and length
more in it than above it

the ancient child asks
how should you lead the world around you

by example
without trying to control the common details of living

contending causes contention
have no part of it

CHAPTER SIXTY-SEVEN

stand in the shape of greatness
with feet resting firmly upon the land
and arms ringed as if holding a large tree
embracing and holding the vastness
of the *tao* source of life

it seems silly that such a simple activity
can bring you to greatness
but it can

in fact
if it didn't appear silly and simple
it would not be worth it
at all

stand in the shape of greatness
radiating a mother's love for all the world
restraining the outflowing of your lifeforce
remaining vigilant and aware of the world's momentum

for a mother's love is selfless and fearless
restrained lifeforce is amplified until needed
and vigilance will help you avoid the knives
that are all around you

for true greatness to present itself
moderation is the key

being too compassionate in your life
being too generous with your life
being the leader who saves everyone else's life
will end your own
before its time

a mother's love is an impenetrable fortress
a mother's love is an unstoppable weapon

stand in the shape of greatness
with a mother's love
and heaven will flow into you

CHAPTER SIXTY-EIGHT

a true warrior is not deliberately belligerent
and does not show off his fighting skills

a true warrior is a gentle man
and does not lose his temper

a true warrior is not entangled in the trivial
and does not need to win arguments

a true warrior
does not look or act like
a true warrior

but he is a true warrior
possessed of an ancient virtue
that is non-contentious and sublime

under heaven
he knows how to unite himself
with heaven
peacefully complying with the principles
of heaven

a true warrior
stands firm

Chapter Sixty-nine

it is difficult to understand the need
for a warrior under heaven
but conflict is a fact of life
that lies at the heart of conflict's absence

peace

so you must behave like a warrior
when a warrior is needed

the ancient child asks
how do you behave like a warrior

act as a defender and not as an invader
march forward without appearing to march forward
be lazy about tying up your war coat
utilize a war hand only as needed
use your empty hand before drawing a sword
be measured and resolute in battle
even though you would rather abstain

the greatest harm you can do is to
treat your opponent lightly

give him his due and win the day
or you will lose touch with your inner world

when two opposing forces meet
and do combat
the one that is compassionate and yielding
will surely conquer
the other

Chapter Seventy

the ancient child asks
can you keep my teachings
everything I am saying to you
both my words and what they teach
are very easy to understand and put into practice
yet so few people on this planet
are able to do so

the ancient child says
complicating my teachings will turn them to nothing

the ancient child commands
speak for me

my words and what they teach are a time-binding song
with ancient roots and an infinite length

my corporeal actions reveal a time-bound method
that seeks to keep me aligned with the universe

my words and my actions are so oblique
that logical attempts at understanding me are futile

knowing   me   not   me   knowing

know me by not knowing me
and I become clear and rare to you

know me by not knowing me
and I will appear elegant and sacred to you

know me by not knowing me
and I will open my precious heart to you

CHAPTER SEVENTY-ONE

knowing by not knowing is an unconscious understanding
that exists subtly as transcendent and lofty

it is revealed knowledge
that flows with ease from within

all the knowledge of the universe can be sensed
at the corner of your senses
locked away inside each and every cell of your bodymind

getting to it requires
that you flow with ease from within

trying to understand the subtle and transcendent
consciously
will put you in a state of
dis-ease
blocking the flow from within

CHAPTER SEVENTY-TWO

treat yourself with respect as you cultivate the *tao* way of life

authentic wisdom as revealed knowledge
can become overpowering and make you afraid
because its implications are profound and far-reaching

the force of revealed knowledge
can sometimes make you feel small and insignificant
push you to austerity and
make you feel undeserving

the sage wise man is not afraid
and is content to be overpowered

know that you are vast and significant
deserving of all the good things that life has to offer
and life will always be at your fingertips

Chapter Seventy-three

do not be reckless with your life
blind courage and blind passion can kill you
however
courage and passion informed by revealed knowledge
can fill you with abundant lifeforce

one is for life
one is for death

the force of heaven flowing with ease
through a bodymind cultivating the *tao* way of life
overcomes any obstacle and sustains that bodymind

the force of heaven flowing with ease
speaks without words and answers questions
before they are complete

the force of heaven flowing with ease
can be summoned by only a gentle invitation
and a door left open

the force of heaven flowing with ease
appears spontaneous while
acting according to a divine plan

the force of heaven flowing with ease
through a bodymind cultivating the *tao* way of life
appears unhurried and unworried
peaceful and delicate

its comings and goings are blessings
that are beyond your control

heaven's net is a gossamer web covering the world
connecting every single thing under it
to every other single thing under it

think of things in this way
and you will become
the force of heaven flowing with ease

Chapter Seventy-four

if you believe in the literal impossibility of death
you will not fear dying
and life will always be available to you

if you fear death
you will become fearful of life
and
complicated situations
perverse thinking
bizarre events
dishonest behavior and
deceitful people
will bind your hands and be at your throat

the ancient child asks
who are the bodymind killers

complicated situations
perverse thinking
bizarre events
dishonest behavior
deceitful people

these things drain away your lifeforce
causing accidents and injury
to every one around you
no matter how able and resilient you may be

CHAPTER SEVENTY-FIVE

requiting the bodymind killers
takes too much energy
and starves you for living

a starving bodymind rebels and acts unruly

knowing it can not easily die
it makes you sick, heavy, and anxious
attempting to grab your attention
entreating you to listen to its cries

a living bodymind asks you to get out of its way
and let it live

Chapter Seventy-six

the ancient child asks
how do you get out of the bodymind's way and let it live

by allowing your soul to take the lead of your life

the ancient child asks
how do you let the soul take the lead of your life

be as gentle and tender as a newborn
soft, yielding, supple, and full of lifeforce

avoid stiffness, rigidity, and naked force

emulate the living things of the world delicately
and at a distance

avoid hardening your bodymind and spirit
avoid those unyielding things that stink of decay

embody those things that are tender and pliant
which grant life and freedom

avoid mustering your talents and collecting your strengths
in a forceful or headstrong manner

remember
an unyielding tree will snap under a strong wind
or fall easily under a dull ax

pattern yourself after a great tree
with deep roots and strong branches
and you will exalt your bodymind and spirit

Chapter Seventy-seven

bend the bow and embrace the tiger
to emulate the way of heaven

drawn with resoluteness
the bow changes length and width
turning in on itself

released with resoluteness
the bow projects its arrow fixedly to a target
by equalizing itself

the bow can shoot up or down as needed
always seeking to balance out
flexibility and cohesion
always seeking to resolve
excesses of energy and deficiencies of energy

equalizing and balancing out and resolving
are the ways of heaven

but the ways of man
make things unequal
imbalanced and unresolved
cutting man off from heaven and earth

only a sage wise man humbly cultivating the *tao* way of life
can entreat heaven on man's behalf
asking heaven
to reestablish the natural order
by not asking heaven

when he is successful
he does not dwell on it
displaying his skill at emulating the way of heaven

he simply smiles
and moves on to the next task

CHAPTER SEVENTY-EIGHT

remember
to be at your best
pattern yourself after water

nothing in all the world is softer or more powerful
nothing in all the world can substitute for it
nothing in all the world can stop it

in their hearts
everyone easily knows that
the soft and weak
will always overcome the hard and strong
but they find it difficult to live this way

the secret is to
move the bodymind like water

Chapter Seventy-nine

harmonizing great resentments and injuries
requires a soft but steady equilibrium

but even in a gentle balancing of the scales
some friction and pain will always remain

harmony can still be reached
if the sage wise man doesn't push
for complete unity

the sage wise man comes to understand that flawless justice
is impossible
so he holds an even temperament instead

great knowledge comes from the left hand
holding something broken and flawed

accept the small inequities

a bodymind embracing the *tao* way of life
doesn't need perfection
a bodymind rejects the *tao* way of life
striving for perfection

remember
heaven lends its strength to those who
follow the natural laws of the universe

Chapter Eighty

keep your life simple and interesting

striving for great talent and skill
striving for great and perfect tools
is not the true way

have just enough talent
have just enough skill
have just the right amount of tools for work
have just the right amount of weapons for protection

the ancient child asks
how much is the right amount

know one hundred songs
so you can play a single simple melody
from the heart
to a heart

treat complex things
as simple things
arranged in a pattern
that
once you are at peace
can be easily deciphered

remember your ancient roots
read your history
relish your food
revel in your habits and customs
rest in your home
return to the tried and true

place great value in the natural order
of life and death

do not wander far from home

play and have fun in your life
and your back yard
will become a world
that will take you a lifetime to explore

what could be better

CHAPTER EIGHTY-ONE

words that communicate success
are not complex and showy

they are simple and direct

words that transform the bodymind
are not adorned and fancy

they are plain and well-placed

words that speak of the *tao* source and way of life
are open and few

words born of the union of perception and preception
are not true words at all

true words are silent

the sage wise man does not live to accumulate
instead
he lives to help people
because the sage wise man realizes that
how he behaves towards others
is really
how he behaves towards himself
and the universe

he is in harmony with the *tao* source and way of life

because
as man
he stands with outstretched bodymind and hands
between heaven
and earth